J B CROCKETT 2020
Furstinger, Nancy
Davy Crockett

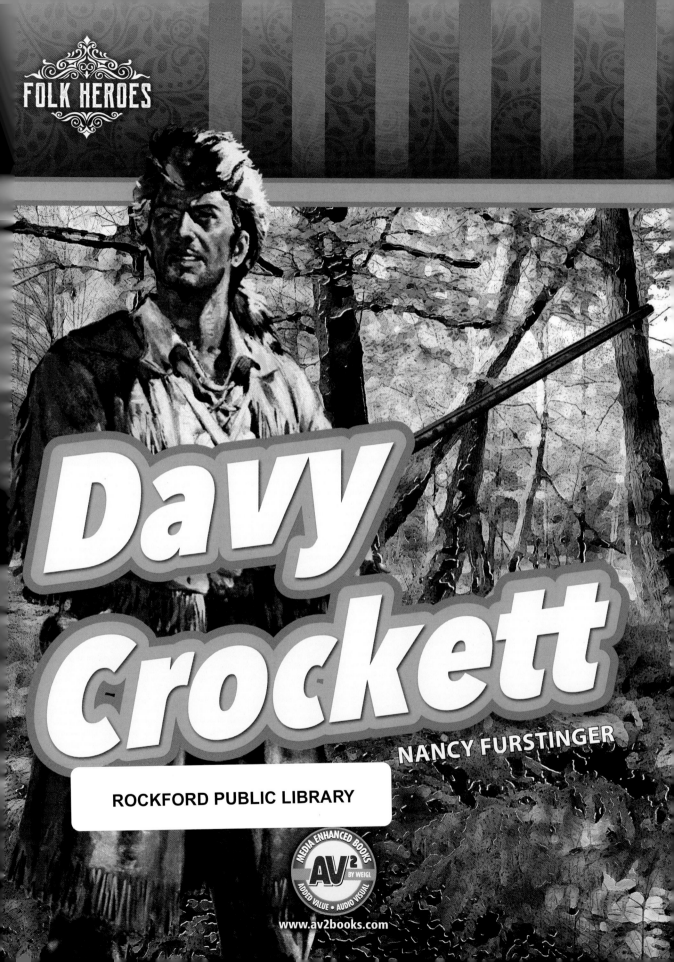

FOLK HEROES

Davy Crockett

NANCY FURSTINGER

MEDIA ENHANCED BOOKS
AV2 BY WEIGL
ADDED VALUE • AUDIO VISUAL

www.av2books.com

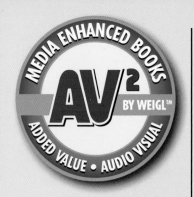

AV² provides enriched content that supplements and complements this book. Weigl's AV² books strive to create inspired learning and engage young minds in a total learning experience.

Your AV² Media Enhanced books come alive with...

Audio
Listen to sections of the book read aloud.

Key Words
Study vocabulary, and complete a matching word activity.

Video
Watch informative video clips.

Quizzes
Test your knowledge.

Embedded Weblinks
Gain additional information for research.

Slide Show
View images and captions, and prepare a presentation.

Try This!
Complete activities and hands-on experiments.

... and much, much more!

Go to **www.av2books.com**, and enter this book's unique code.

BOOK CODE

A V C 8 5 6 4 2

AV² by Weigl brings you media enhanced books that support active learning.

Published by AV² by Weigl
350 5th Avenue, 59th Floor
New York, NY 10118
Website: www.av2books.com

Library of Congress Cataloging-in-Publication Data
Names: Furstinger, Nancy, author.
Title: Davy Crockett / Nancy Furstinger.
Description: New York, NY : AV2 by Weigl, [2019] | Series: Folk heroes | Includes index. | Audience: Grades 4-6.
Identifiers: LCCN 2018051728 (print) | LCCN 2018052174 (ebook) | ISBN 9781489695666 (Multi User ebook)
 | ISBN 9781489695673 (Single User ebook) | ISBN 9781489695475 (hardcover : alk. paper) | ISBN 9781489695482 (softcover : alk. paper)
Subjects: LCSH: Crockett, Davy, 1786-1836--Juvenile literature. |
 Pioneers--Tennessee--Biography--Juvenile literature. | Frontier and pioneer life--Tennessee--Juvenile literature. |
 Tennessee--Biography--Juvenile literature. | Legislators--United States--Biography--Juvenile literature.
Classification: LCC F436.C95 (ebook) | LCC F436.C95 F87 2018 (print) | DDC
 976.8/04092 [B] --dc23
LC record available at https://lccn.loc.gov/2018051728

Printed in Guangzhou, China
1 2 3 4 5 6 7 8 9 0 23 22 21 20 19

012019
130118

Project Coordinator: Heather Kissock
Art Director: Terry Paulhus

Photo Credits
Every reasonable effort has been made to trace ownership and to obtain permission to reprint copyright material. The publishers would be pleased to have any errors or omissions brought to their attention so that they may be corrected in subsequent printings.

Weigl acknowledges Getty Images, Alamy, and Bridgeman Images as its primary image suppliers for this title.

Davy Crockett

CONTENTS

A Friendly Frontiersman

Davy Crockett was a popular American **frontiersman**. People told wild stories about his strength and skills. People also knew that Davy was a good hunter. Some of these stories became legends, which are stories that cannot be proven to be true. These stories helped Davy become a folk hero.

Davy could barely read or write, but he worked successfully in the government. He did not use fancy words in his speeches. Instead, he spoke plainly and used the same language as other people in the community. His speeches made him popular with the people.

It was said that Davy was so strong that he once ripped the tail off a **comet**.

Davy Crockett is often referred to as the "King of the Wild Frontier."

Davy Crockett

Davy was born just outside the town of Limestone. In 1973, David Crockett Birthplace State Park was established in his honor.

Growing Up

Davy Crockett was born on August 17, 1786, in Greene County, Tennessee. Davy's parents struggled to make enough money for the family. Their nine children needed food and clothing. By the time Davy was 8 years old, he was helping feed his family by hunting **game**.

To help earn money, Davy's father sent him to herd cattle in Virginia. When he returned, Davy was involved in a fight at school. Davy did not go back to school after the fight. He ran away from home because he was afraid that his father would punish him. Davy did not return home for 3 years.

Davy worked for a **Quaker** farmer when he was 16 years old. He worked 2 days each week in exchange for 4 days of schooling. He studied reading, writing, and mathematics. Davy studied for 100 days. He hoped this knowledge would attract a wife.

Crockett's Career

D avy Crockett became a government worker in 1817. As a justice of the peace, he acted as a judge for his community. In 1821, Davy became a member of the Tennessee **legislature**. Six years later, he was elected to Congress. He served there for three terms. When Davy tried for a fourth term in Congress, he lost the election.

Davy became popular and respected. Many people thought he had a good sense of humor. Davy was also known for always fighting for what he believed in.

"Be always sure you are right, then go ahead."

Davy Crockett's **motto**

Davy's skills as a storyteller were of great help to him during his political career.

The attack on Fort Mims took place on August 30, 1813. More than 250 men, women, and children were either killed or captured.

American Shooter

Davy was skilled at shooting guns. His great aim won many local shooting contests. Davy and his competitors paid 25 cents each for one shot at a target. Davy often won all of the prizes because he was the best shooter.

Davy joined the **militia** when the **Creek** attacked Fort Mims in Alabama. He shot bears for food for the soldiers. In 1825, he shot 105 black bears. Stories say that Davy once shot seventeen black bears in a week.

"I took a notion to hunt a little more, and in about one month I killed forty-seven more..."

– Davy Crockett

The Look of a Legend

Davy Crockett was an imposing figure. He stood about 6 feet (1.8 meters) tall and weighed about 200 pounds (91 kilograms). Davy liked to tell people that he was a blend of horse, alligator, and snapping turtle. What he really meant was that he was strong and brave. Davy boasted that he could "ride a streak of lightning." These **tall tales** helped to spread his fame as a folk hero.

Think About It

People's clothing can say a great deal about them. What do Davy's clothes say about him? Why was it important for him to carry a knife? How did his clothes affect his hunting ability? What would you wear if you lived in the 1800s? Think about why each clothing item would be important to a frontiersman.

Davy always wore his **coonskin** cap. The cap protected his head from the hot sun. The raccoon's tail hung down Davy's back. People recognized Davy because of his coonskin cap.

Davy began hunting with a long rifle when he was very young. Davy nicknamed his rifle Betsy.

Davy wore a fringed, deerskin hunting shirt. His shirt and leggings were tanned. Tanning made the deerskin soft and prevented it from rotting. It also helped the clothing to dry faster.

Davy often traveled with his Bowie knife. This was a long, sharp, steel hunting knife.

Deerskin **moccasins** helped Davy to move silently through the forests. The soft material allowed Davy to feel dry twigs under his feet. This stopped him from stepping on twigs and making noise.

The Battle of the Alamo lasted for 13 days. James, Davy, and the Texan volunteers were unsuccessful in their efforts to defend the fort. The Mexican forces took control of it on March 6, 1836.

Friend and Foe

Davy clashed with Andrew Jackson when Andrew became the president. Davy did not agree with the president's plan to move the Native Americans to land on the west side of the Mississippi River. Davy also did not want Andrew to sell land to rich people instead of the **settlers**, who he felt deserved the land.

In 1835, Davy took his rifle to the Texas frontier. He joined the Texans who were battling for independence from Mexico. Davy fought under the direction of James Bowie. James invented the knife that bears his name.

James led the volunteers into battle at the Alamo, a fort in San Antonio. Both James and Davy died at the Alamo, along with about 187 Texans and 600 Mexicans.

James Bowie

Crockett Continues

Davy became a hero once again in a Disney television series that was called *Davy Crockett*. The show aired in 1954, and was an instant success. Children watched their hero river raft and fight at the Alamo. Coonskin caps became popular gifts.

Today, people travel to the log cabin at David Crockett Birthplace State Park in Limestone, Tennessee. The cabin is similar to the one Davy was born in. Stepping inside the cabin feels like stepping back in time. In East Texas, visitors can also spend time in the 160,000-acre (64,750-hectare) Davy Crockett National Forest. People can swim, canoe, and hike while they are visiting the forest.

In 1955, a recording of "The Ballad of Davy Crockett," the television show's theme song, was released. Ten million records of the song were sold.

The Disney TV show ran from 1954 to 1955. An actor named Fess Parker played Davy.

Timeline of Davy Crockett

1786
Davy Crockett is born in Greene County, Tennessee.

1806
Davy marries Mary "Polly" Finley.

1813
Davy joins the Tennessee Volunteer Militia and fights in the Creek War. This war is fought between settlers and Native Americans over land.

1802
Davy works two days each week in exchange for four days of schooling at a Quaker farm.

1798
Davy herds cattle across 400 miles of land in Virginia.

1827
Davy is elected to work for Congress. He serves three terms.

Davy Crockett lived a full and active life. From his rural roots, he rose to become a soldier, politician, and frontiersman. His many exploits earned Davy a larger-than-life reputation. He became one of the country's best-known folk heroes as a result.

1821
Davy is elected to the state legislature at 35 years of age.

1828
Davy fights for the Land Bill. The bill would let frontier settlers purchase land at low cost.

1835
Davy tries to be elected to Congress a fourth time. He loses the election and travels to Texas.

 1836

Davy dies at the Alamo. He was helping Texas fight for independence from Mexico.

1

In which state did Davy herd cattle?

a) Texas
b) Virginia
c) Tennessee
d) Alabama

2

Which animal was Davy's famous cap made from?

a) bear
b) deer
c) possum
d) raccoon

What Have You Learned?

Test your knowledge of Davy Crockett by answering the following questions.

3

What was one thing Davy and President Andrew Jackson disagreed about?

a) the moving of Native Americans
b) Davy's lack of education
c) killing bears
d) defending the Alamo

4

True or False?
Davy is often referred to as the "King of the Wild West."

5

True or False?
Davy's motto was:
"Be always sure you
are right, then go ahead."

6

True or False?
Davy named his
rifle Jenny.

7

True or False?
Davy was born in Texas.

8

True or False?
Davy won many
prizes for shooting
in local contests.

10

True or False?
Davy wore boots when he
was hunting.

9

True or False?
Davy died
in Tennessee
after fighting
in the Battle
of the Alamo.

Truth or Legend?

It is often hard to separate Davy Crockett's real story from the larger-than-life legends. This American frontier hero is still popular after hundreds of years. Storytellers have claimed that Davy killed a bear when he was only 3 years old. We know that this is impossible. Davy did hunt 105 bears in 6 months. Pick an event from your life and create a fictional story about it. Design a book cover to illustrate your story. Then, share your story with friends and classmates.

Key Words

comet: an object in space that looks like a star with a tail of light

coonskin: the fur of a raccoon

Creek: a Native-American group

frontiersman: a person who lives or travels in an undeveloped area

game: wild animals hunted for sport, money, or food

legislature: the branch of government that makes and changes laws

militia: citizens who are trained to help fight in emergencies

moccasins: soft shoes made of animal skins

motto: a short sentence that says what someone believes in

Quaker: member of a Christian religious group, which was founded in England; the Quakers believe in peace

settlers: people who move to a new country to make their homes

tall tales: exaggerated stories

Index

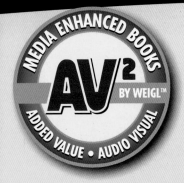

Log on to www.av2books.com

AV² by Weigl brings you media enhanced books that support active learning. Go to www.av2books.com, and enter the special code found on page 2 of this book. You will gain access to enriched and enhanced content that supplements and complements this book. Content includes video, audio, weblinks, quizzes, a slideshow, and activities.

AV² Online Navigation

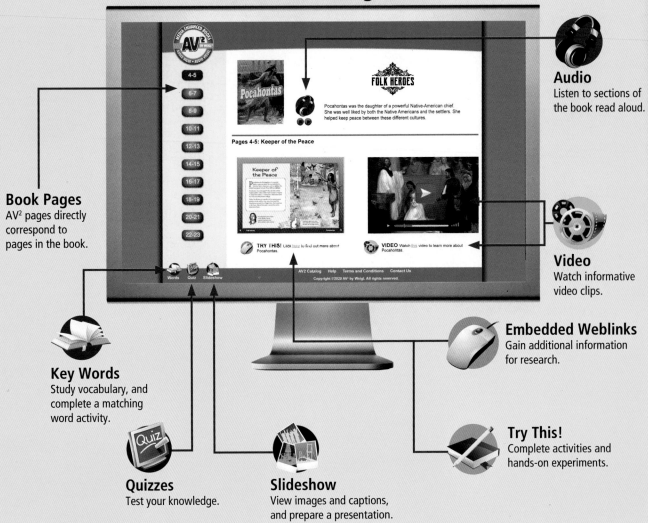

Audio
Listen to sections of the book read aloud.

Video
Watch informative video clips.

Book Pages
AV² pages directly correspond to pages in the book.

Embedded Weblinks
Gain additional information for research.

Key Words
Study vocabulary, and complete a matching word activity.

Try This!
Complete activities and hands-on experiments.

Quizzes
Test your knowledge.

Slideshow
View images and captions, and prepare a presentation.

AV² was built to bridge the gap between print and digital. We encourage you to tell us what you like and what you want to see in the future.

Sign up to be an AV² Ambassador at www.av2books.com/ambassador.